HUSTLE &
FAITH

god honors your faith and rewards your hustle!

MARCUS D. WILEY

ISBN: 978-1-60414-839-8

Edited by Leah Davis & Dawn Jenkins
Scripture quotation used from King James Version

Published in Houston, Texas, by
Wileywood Entertainment

WWW.MARCUSDWILEY.COM

PRINTED IN THE UNITED STATES OF AMERICA

TABLE OF CONTENTS

Foreword by Yolanda Adams............................. *v*

Introduction .... *ix*

Chapter 1   4th Ward 1

Chapter 2   This Is It 7

Chapter 3   Thank You Joe 11

Chapter 4   Angelina Community College 21

Chapter 5   Why Not Us 29

Chapter 6   Erica 37

Chapter 7   Wileywood.................................... 47

Chapter 8   Show Me the Money 53

Chapter 9   All God Says I Am........................ 61

Chapter 10   The Point Of It All 73

Chapter 11   Hustle Highlights & Hardships 79

Chapter 12   Can You Hear Me Now 85

Acknowledgements................................. *94*

FOREWORD

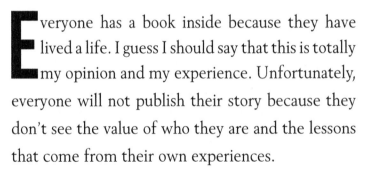

Everyone has a book inside because they have lived a life. I guess I should say that this is totally my opinion and my experience. Unfortunately, everyone will not publish their story because they don't see the value of who they are and the lessons that come from their own experiences.

We all have read about people who've done amazing things and probably thought, "Man, I went through something almost identical to so-and-so." The only difference between you and so-and-so is, the determination to get the story out of your experience and onto printed pages or electronic readers.

I remembered mentioning to Marcus that he should make a movie of his journey in the entertainment industry. Too often, people embark on the journey and get easily dismayed when things don't turn out as rosy as their dreams.

In their dreams, they meet someone who says, "Hey Kid, you got the goods" and BAM, they're a Star!!! But as the title of this outstanding book tells us, we have to put a little Hustle to our Faith. *Hustle and Faith* is not just the title of this book; it is literally Marcus' way of life.

For the past 9 years, I've had the privilege of working side by side with Marcus D. Wiley in various aspects of the entertainment business. He is a multi-talented, multi-faceted, young man whose faith is so balanced that many miss the depth of it. He cleverly mixes urban vernacular and church lingo with such brilliance even youngsters understand the gist of his delivery.

I love being a witness of process and progress. Journaling, to me, is an example of both. You are engaged in the writing process while inscribing your progress. Marcus has often joked about my colorful way of journaling. I told him that he does the same thing every morning without the different colored pens.

When I explained why I did it, I saw a bulb of enlightenment turn on almost like the animated ones in cartoons. You see, Marcus writes every joke and benchmark segment he does on the Morning Show. I get a chance to see "Genius in Action" daily. Let's push all my corny jokes aside. This book is an inspiration to anyone who reads it. Marcus makes you want to read his story to the very end.

He takes you step by step, like a tour guide, through parts of his life, and not all parts are "Jokey-Jokey." However, his intent is to bring you into an awareness of how he views his life and his GOD. As a believer in Divine Purpose, Marcus also shows you that when it gets hard, dig deeper and hustle a little more.

So I invite you to sit back with your favorite cup or glass of whatever and spend a couple of hours with Professor Marcus D. Wiley. His Hustle will encourage you. His Faith will astound you. But more than anything, you will feel like a close friend of this Man of Purpose. ENJOY!

~Yolanda Adams

INTRODUCTION

I wouldn't go to church every Sunday, go to Bible study every Wednesday and only believe some of the scriptures. What's the point or purpose of learning, believing and quoting scripture if you're not going to live it? I'm not talking about all of it, meaning the entire 66 books; but at least live some of it! I encourage people to find a hand full of scriptures you're going to believe in, stand on and gamble with. Okay not gamble, but roll with.

My favorite scripture in the Bible is Romans 8:28, "All things work together for the good of those who love the Lord and are called according to His purpose". I believe this one scripture has shaped my entire perspective on life. *Hustle and Faith* is not the book that is going to change your life. *Hustle and Faith* is a testimony of how my life changed. A wonderful change has come over me! It's my prayer that the readers will be able to identify, relate to and begin to self-evaluate, if you're doing your part in creating your change.

So many people email me, tweet me, Facebook me, call me or come up to me asking me how did I get where I am today. I tell them, I did my part and God did his part! What I'm getting ready to say is probably blasphemous, but stay with me. Just believing in God will not get you what you want in life. It's a fantastic start! Congratulations, if you are saved, but if you're not working towards what you believe, do you really believe?

Hustle and Faith is a book of factual stories. Now, Webster's definition of *hustle* is to work rapidly, to energetically press to accomplish a task or goal. The Marcus D. Wiley definition of hustle goes something to the tune of, showing God how bad I want it!

God honors your faith and rewards your hustle! For so long, the word hustle has been looked at as negative, but it is what all Christians should be doing! In church, they teach us the importance of faith and constantly tell us to just believe. For if we just believe in God, everything is going to work for your good. I wanted to believe the pastor when he would say this, I really did, but I always felt there was more to it. Yeah, the crowd would go wild and the church would explode and breakout into a radical praise about the blessings they were promised. However, weeks, months and even years later, those blessings would never manifest. As suspected, believing you receive is only the first part. There are other parts missing and I believe the missing parts are the reason why so many Christians fail to experience God's best.

"That the blessing of Abraham might come on the Gentiles through Jesus Christ; that we might receive the promise of the Spirit through faith." ~ Galatians 3:14

Now Galatians 3:14 says that the promise of the Spirit is received by faith. So it's safe to say, all of God's promises are received by faith. So in order to have God's best in your life, you've got to have faith. What is this faith stuff all about anyway? I did some investigating. Hebrews 11:1 says "Faith is the substance of things hoped for and the evidence of things not seen". If I were to add in my two cents, I'd define faith as, having enough confidence in God, to act on what you believe. James 2:17 says "Faith without works is dead." That basically means you can believe all day long, but if YOU are not working for your good, why should God. Your faith needs a job, an assignment, a target and until you put it to work, you will never see the benefits package God has for you.

When I read the Bible, I noticed that there are several examples of people who had faith. If they could just get to Jesus, He would change their situation. Remember the lady with the issue of blood in Luke 8:43? She "pressed" her way through the crowd and touched the hem of his garment, and because of her faith she was made whole. In the parable of the talents, the master gave one man 5 talents, another 2 talents, and the other 1 talent.

The man with 5 talents hustled and got 10, the man with 2 talents hustled and got 4, but the man with one talent hid his talent. When the master returned, he called the man who hid his talent, lazy. He took his talent and gave it to the hustler with 10. And how can we forget the paralyzed man in Mark 2 whose friends cut a hole in Jesus' roof just to get their friend before the Lord. Wow! That took faith and guts; good thing Jesus was a carpenter.

I can go on and on with biblical examples of *hustle* and *faith*. Even the twelve guys Jesus picked to lead the kingdom agenda were not saints or scholars. The text says they were normal men who had steady jobs. In other words, they were working. There's something about people who work, hustle and are out there getting it that He likes. While you are waiting on God to show up, He's waiting on you to get up, get out and do something!

CHAPTER 1

4TH WARD

t's two o'clock in the morning and I'm in a deep coma-like sleep. My grandfather, Andrew Wiley, Sr., wakes me up, not because the house is on fire, but because we have to go across the street to Albert Woods Café to collect beer cans.

Never mind the fact I'm only seven years old, I've got school in the morning, I've already taken a bath, I'm smelling like Sure deodorant and Johnson and Johnson baby powder. My grandfather still picks me up and puts me in the dumpster. This was my first lesson in "hustling."

I grew up in 4th Ward, Texas, an inner city neighborhood of Houston. I lived in a three bedroom, one bathroom panel house, with my grandparents, Andrew and Ruth Wiley; my aunts, Linda, known as Teeny; and Sandra, known as Poochie; my Uncle Larry, known as Bo; and my Mama, Brenda. Though it was very crowded in the house, there was lots of love, laughter and loaning of money. I remember nothing but having very good times there.

Our house was cater-cornered to a juke joint, a hole in the wall called Albert Woods Cafe. I went to bed every night listening to the sounds of rhythm and blues. I believe this is where my distinct love for music came about. Our walls were so thin, you could hear Earth, Wind, and Fire, The O'Jays, Teddy Pendergrass, etc. loud and clear through the walls, as if they were singing right in the house every night.

There were six wards in Houston. 4th Ward was the first ward built and people wonder why I struggle in math. I loved 4th Ward, but 4th Ward was loud! Ambulances, sirens, children playing, ice cream trucks, domestic arguments and occasional gunshots were the soundtrack of our lives. I remember playing at Wiley Park until the streetlights came on.

Though the park had nothing to do with my family name, I told everybody we owned it. I lived right down the street from the candy lady. You know, the lady that sold cool cups, tea cakes and candy cheaper than the corner store; but be careful she had cats.

My grandfather was a baggage claims man for Southern Pacific Railroad and Chairman of the Trustee Board at Macedonia Missionary Baptist Church. The cans were supplemental income to his regular income. When you're the head of a household with seven people in it, relying on a single income is not an option. You got to get out and get it. In other words, you've got to hustle!

Everybody in 4th Ward was hustling. Hustling until they got their next check. Hustling the government out of checks. Hustling on the corner. Hustling just to get by. Hustling for a ride. Hustling just to hustle.

There were various types of hustlers in 4th Ward:

- **LAZY HUSTLER:** living off the government, section 8, food stamps

3

- **SLICK HUSTLER:** overcharge you for things

- **OPPORTUNISTIC HUSTLER:** looking to come up with a lawsuit

- **GIGOLO HUSTLER:** a man who pleasures women to get what he wants

- **GOLD DIGGING HUSTLER:** a woman who pleasures men to get what she wants

- **ILLEGAL HUSTLER:** selling drugs, stolen goods, etc.

- **WORKAHOLIC HUSTLER:** has a full-time job plus works multiple side jobs to pay the bills

Everybody in 4th ward was hustling for one purpose and that was to make ends meet, connect or at least come close. Everybody's main goal was to get it anyway you could. Everyone was operating in panic mode. Get food or starve, pay rent or get evicted, rob or get robbed, hustle or die. No need to utilize faith at this point. Faith requires patience and waiting on God. No one in 4th Ward had time for that! We need a miracle now!

I grew up hearing people say, "When I become an adult, I will get a good job." I rarely heard anyone say, "I should go to college," but I did hear people say, "I should get a good job." These good jobs were, for example, working at the post office or a good city job with benefits or working for the railroad, like my grandfather.

Now, before you say, "Where's his daddy?" my biological father's name is Dave Botts, Jr. He lived with my other grandparents, Pastor David and Anna Lee Botts, in South Acres, Texas. My father had tons of charisma. He was a charmer and a smooth talker. He was also a quartet singer (and still is).

I would get so excited when he was coming to pick me up. One particular time he was supposed to come get me and it was storming. I sat on the porch with my bag waiting. Every car that passed by; I thought it was him. I would get up and go call the house. He wasn't at home. So, surely he was on his way to get me. Finally, when it got dark, my mama told me to come in the house. "Boy, yo daddy not coming."

He showed up two days later and asked me was I ready to go. I told him, "I'm not going."

He asked me, "Why not?"

I told him, "Because you were supposed to pick me up two days ago."

He said, "It was storming outside."

And I said, "But you weren't at home."

My mama took up for me and told me if I didn't want to go, I didn't have to go. This experience taught me a valuable lesson. I'll never let bad weather stop me from doing something I want to do. If I plan on barbecuing and it starts raining, I'll put up a tent and carry on as planned. The book of New Edition says, "sunny days…everybody loves them, but tell me can you stand the rain?" Since I can't change the weather, I'm not going to let the weather change me!

CHAPTER 2

THIS IS IT

I was a normal kid. I rode skateboards, big wheels, green machines, and bikes. I played hide and seek, Simon says, mother may I, and 123 red light. I played dodge ball, kick ball, football, baseball, and basketball. I even played house with the girls, LOL.

However, I remember the day I knew what I wanted to do for the rest of my life. I was in the fifth grade. We were having a Black History program at Gregory Lincoln Elementary. It was around the time when Michael Jackson's "Thriller" was released and everyone was talking about the video. We didn't have cable at my house, so I didn't get to see the video when it was first aired on MTV. One of my classmate's daddies was good with wires, so they had illegal cable at their house. They also had a hot VCR that his daddy bought from the local Walmart known as the "barbershop". He was able to tape the video and bring it to school.

My class thought I should be Mike! Me? Michael Jackson? I remember watching the "Thriller" video and studying MJ's moves. We made tombstones out of cardboards and put dry ice in pans behind it so the smoke would be flowing during our performance. My classmates that were performing wore ripped clothes because they were dead bodies that were now alive.

However, I was MJ! I had to be fresh! I already knew if momma was going to have to buy me something to wear, I would have to resign as Michael Jackson. We didn't have money to play with so I had to be creative. I already had a pair of jeans that were too short. I had some white church socks, white t-shirt, and I had a white usherboard glove. The problem was the jacket and the penny loafers! I ended up wearing a pair of my black church shoes and one of my classmates let me wear his Black Members Only jacket!

The auditorium was packed! All the students, faculty, staff, parents, siblings and friends were in the building. I was nervous as all get out! I made a mistake and peeked through the curtains and saw all these people expecting to see Michael Jackson and I went from nervous to scared! And then it happened; the announcer said, "Our next performance will surely be a thriller! Put your hands together for Ms. Hall's fifth grade class, lead by Marcus Wiley doing Michael Jackson's "Thriller". The moment I heard the applause – from the time I felt the energy from the crowd, the anticipation on their faces, and heard all of those girls screaming (most of whom wouldn't even speak to me on a normal school day, but for my performance they were screaming and clapping) I knew at that moment — this is it! I wanted to be an entertainer. I was hooked and totally bit by the entertainment bug. I wanted to feel that energy all the time and make people happy.

The beauty of entertaining is: you have a room full of people from all different walks of life; different experiences; frames of reference and opinions. A room full of people with their own mind and probably thinking about all the noise going on in their lives, but for however long I'm on the stage, I have the opportunity to get everybody in the room to leave their world and come to my world.

I'm responsible for your attention. I don't take it for granted.

As a fifth grader, I had no idea of the hustle, bustle and determination it took to make it in the entertainment industry and I didn't care. All I knew was this was the life I wanted. I released my faith for it, I declared it, believed it in my heart, God heard me and now, it was on!

CHAPTER 3

THANK YOU, JOE

The summer after I graduated from elementary school, my mom married a pastor by the name of Joe Jack Culton. This man was not only a pastor, but the pastor of the church we were attending. My entire family attended Macedonia Missionary Baptist Church, but my fast mama attended Peaceful Rest Missionary Baptist Church. I knew something was going on between my mama and the pastor, but I was a kid, and back then, you stayed in a child's place.

I remember one time he took us home from church, and I peeped in the front seat and saw them holding hands. I didn't think she was supposed to be holding the pastor's hand. I thought maybe they were touching and agreeing. Nevertheless, they got married on September 1, 1984 and like Prince Charming, Joe sent a limousine to come pick us up from 4th ward.

The only time you saw a limo in 4th Ward was for a funeral. But this limo was coming to take us to our new life. My mom and I were a package deal. Joe never treated me like a step-son and I never treated him like a step-dad.

My mom made sure I knew who my biological daddy was and who my "real" daddy was. I say, if he really loves your momma, really takes care of the bills and really supports you...that's not your step daddy that's your real daddy. Biological parents create you, but real parents raise you.

We moved to our new home in a place called Missouri City, Texas, which is a suburb right outside of Houston. Mo City was the bomb. We had an all brick house. I had my own room with my own phone. The neighborhood was quiet. I was so used to noise; it was scary quiet. It's crazy how when you're so use to chaos, peace will scare you! People in Missouri City were successful and they were hustling on another level. Instead of hustling to get, they were hustling to maintain what they had.

I began to meet black lawyers, doctors and engineers, which was a definite change from what I saw in the "hood". One thing I learned about moving out of the "hood" is everybody is not happy for you when you leave them behind. Going back to 4th Ward became a burden. We got crucified for having what I thought everyone in the "hood" wanted…a better life.

Since I was now officially a preacher's kid, this meant I was going to be in church all of the time. I went to church three times a week: on Tuesdays, Saturdays and all day Sundays. I learned a lot about God and became very active in church. I worked in almost every ministry at the church. I was in the choir, an usher, a deacon, in the brotherhood, a Sunday school teacher, and the drummer for the male chorus. You name it, I can claim I've done it in church.

Pastor Culton also allowed me to be very active in school. I played basketball, was an athletic trainer for football and track, was a member of the FBLA (Future Business Leaders of America) and Student Council.

The reverend and I grew closer; I realized this life wasn't going to be so bad after all. He was a man of God but he didn't beat us over the head with the Bible. He would encourage my mom and myself to seek God for ourselves.

I recall asking questions about stories in the Bible and he would respond by saying, "I don't know everything in the Bible! Look it up for yourself." I didn't understand this at first, but I appreciated it as I got older. Now, no one can just tell me something about the Bible. I don't simply take their word for it until I look it up for myself.

I got saved at age 13. I noticed when I started to go to the church, a whole lot of people knew God's Word, but very few were living God's Word. As a matter of fact, it seemed as if they were only words. You would hear people quote, "I'm the head not the tail," and all I see them doing is wagging. "I'm above and not beneath," and all I see is dirt on top of their heads. "I'm the lender and not the borrower." *Well pay me my money back.*

I always wanted to know when were these scriptures I've been hearing about and believed in were actually going to show up and come to fruition. To me, it didn't make sense to be a Christian and constantly say God is good and never experience any of His goodness. This just didn't seem right.

All I know is, somebody was lying and it wasn't God! I already knew the people in the pews were lying, saying they're blessed and it was plain to see they were broke! I was beginning to think the Pastor was lying, teaching us prosperity and giving just to hustle the people out of their tithes and offerings. It wasn't until later I found out what the real issue was. Church folk, at that time, were trained to know the Word, but didn't know how to step out on faith and activate the principles.

So, actually, no one was lying; the people were not lying; God had already blessed us. The preacher wasn't lying; prosperity is our covenant right as believers. The problem was action! Going out and getting it. It's as if God put some money in an account for us, but we would never receive what he has for us until we get up, go to the bank and make a withdrawal.

Back in 4th Ward, you hear the hustler say, "Don't talk about it, be about it." Well done is better than well said. The moral of the story is, Christians talk too much, pray too much and read the Bible too much, when they need to be out there acting on what they talk about, pray about and read about!

FACT #1

"AND"

2 Peter 1:5-9

AND besides this, giving all diligence, add to your faith virtue; AND to virtue knowledge; AND to knowledge temperance; and to temperance patience; AND to patience godliness; AND to godliness brotherly kindness; AND to brotherly kindness charity. For if these things be in you, AND abound, they make you that ye shall neither be barren nor unfruitful in the knowledge of our Lord Jesus Christ. But he that lacketh these things is blind, AND cannot see afar off, AND hath forgotten that he was purged from his old sins.

On the cover of my book there is an AND symbol. The AND symbol is very symbolic. AND means in addition to, along or together with, also, or added to.

So when I hear people say "all you need is faith" — I feel them, but it's a bit misleading.

I remember my mother was teaching the Women's Ministry one day and I sat in the back and listened. She was talking about how God blessed her with a good son. How I graduated from school, stayed out of jail, no babies out of wedlock, didn't get on drugs. I remember thinking, *AND*! Those were all the things I was supposed to do.

The *AND* means something! The *AND* is very important! Can I give you some examples? Peanut butter *AND* jelly, Paul *AND* Silas, husband *AND* wife, Ike *AND* Tina...you get my drift.

In order to be all that God says you can be, you're gonna need to get that AND in your life.

Here, in 2 Peter, we find Simon Peter encouraging the church to remain faithful, but don't just stay there.

The places God is trying to take you. The rooms He wants you in. The stages He wants you on. The people He wants you to touch — you need more than just faith!

So Simon Peter says, have faith, but add to your faith. Its faith AND virtue AND knowledge AND self-control AND perseverance AND godliness. Don't be afraid of the AND.

> 2 Peter 1:9 tells us, *He who lacks these things are shortsighted even to blindness.*

That's why you unravel every time troubles in your way. You fall apart — you shut down — not understanding that your character is being developed.

But for those who have faith AND ... you will neither be barren nor unfruitful.

CHAPTER 4

ANGELINA COMMUNITY COLLEGE

By the time I was a senior at Willowridge High School, I was very popular. I received class awards for most friendly, most unforgettable and wittiest. I was the head student athletic trainer for the football, basketball and track teams.

I was awarded scholarships to a few schools. The biggest scholarship I received was to the University of Texas in Austin. My athletic training coach, Michael John Vara, helped me to get this scholarship.

Though the scholarship was a blessing, my problem was I could not pass the SAT or the ACT college preparatory test. I took the SAT and made a

600 but I needed a 720. People always joke with me saying, "Don't you get 200 points for just putting your name on the test?" So, I took it again and made a 660. My coach suggested that I take the ACT. I made a 16, but an 18 was the required score to be eligible for college.

What was scary about this whole situation was, I was a good student in high school. I graduated with a 3.6 GPA. Out of 660 graduating seniors, I was number 125 but for some strange reason I could not pass these tests. I would pray, but to no avail.

I took the SAT & ACT prep classes, but that didn't work. I blamed myself for not doing well on the tests because they were culturally biased. I had no idea what kayaking, snowboarding and polo were (except for a shirt I couldn't afford) but, I did know what kickball, dodge ball and playing jacks were.

However, I realized that God had a plan for my life and I needed to stay flexible so I didn't get all bent out of shape. There were some things I needed to see, learn and experience. Though I couldn't see it at the time, God was working it all out for my good (Romans 8:28).

Needless to say, I lost those scholarships and ended up going to a junior college in Lufkin, Texas called Angelina Community College, also known as AC.

I honestly thought going to AC was the worst thing ever. The summer after I graduated from high school, I remember running into some of my friends. I asked what colleges they would attend in the fall and they responded with prestigious and profound schools like Notre Dame, USC and Georgetown. They asked me what school was I attending and I'd reluctantly whisper, "Angelina Community College."

They would ask, "Where?" And I would be forced to say Angelina Community College again.

"Where's that?"

"How far away is it?"

"Never heard of it."

As I stated before, I thought going to AC was the worst thing, but it turned out to be the best thing for me. AC taught me three principles that

I live by today — structure, organization, and presentation. Those are the three principles I base my whole life and career on today. In those two years at AC, I can honestly say I grew up.

Being away from home and out of my comfort zone caused me to have to make some decisions in life. I had to decide if I was going to be a thief or not. There was credit card fraud, calling card scams and all types of illegal activities running rampant on the campus. Not to mention, excessive marijuana use, alcohol abuse and the sweet nectar of a woman's fruit.

There were also many different types of hustlers in college. There were people hustling:

Text books
Scholarships
Grants
Test
Cliff notes
Roommates
Line brothers
Line sisters

And let's not forget the infamous credit card companies that were giving out free credit cards to a bunch of students who had no jobs! I had 11 credit cards, by the way, and half of them I didn't even sign up for; they just mysteriously showed up in my mailbox.

I had to make decisions quickly and realize which roads I should take. I saw so many addicts growing up in 4th Ward. There were certain things I just avoided, which automatically made me the designated driver.

Another decision I had to make was if I was going to eat vegetables. I really wasn't a vegetable eater at the time, but when you're in college, hungry and don't have money to buy what you want, you have to eat what's in front of you.

Even though I was far away from home, and living the prodigal life, I still went to church every Sunday. I was used to getting up early on Sunday mornings to go to church. I could party all night, but no matter what time I got in, I was going to church on Sunday morning. It just didn't feel right not going to church on Sundays. I was trained and this was my way of life.

> Proverbs 22:6 says: *"Train up a child in the way he should go: and when he is old, he will not depart from it."*

I had to go to church when I lived at home with my parents. Now, since I didn't *have* to go, I wanted to go. I knew I needed Him and I wouldn't make it without Him. I was on my own and I needed His protection, provision, forgiveness, wisdom, understanding, joy, love and peace. I think this is why today, if I miss church, I'm cool, because I have a better relationship with God now than when I was going to church every Sunday.

I went to a church in Lufkin with my best friend's uncle. We called him Uncle Di. He was a deacon and the church's van driver. He would pick us up on Sunday and after church he would take us to get something to eat at Church's, Popeye's or to his house for Sunday dinner.

His wife would cook like it was Thanksgiving every Sunday. You had a choice of three or four different meats, a bunch of vegetables, desserts and sweet tea. The only bad thing about going to Uncle Di's house is that they were die hard Dallas Cowboy fans.

My roommate at AC was a guy named Lorenzo Ewing. We went to middle school and high school together. He was an all-around good guy and a perfect gentleman. He's the kind of guy you'd let your sister marry. Glad I didn't have one or so I thought!

While we were in college, smack dab in the middle of living la Vida loca, Lorenzo gets called into the ministry. I come home one day to our dorm room, and Lorenzo is on his knees crying. I said, "Bro, what's up?" He tells me he just prayed and God called him to preach the Gospel.

I was like, "But we're just nineteen and in the prime of our lives. Right now, we are gettin' jiggy with it. What are you talking about, the Lord called you? Tell Him to call you back!"

Unfortunately, it was true the Lord called him to preach. This really hurt me because Lo had the look. When we would go to clubs, the girls would flock to him because he was handsome. I had the conversation, he was good looking and together we were a perfect combination. When he was called to preach, he stopped going to the clubs and parties. Now I had to go by myself. See. I kept going, because I am not a quitter. I'm a hustler, Baby!

CHAPTER 5

WHY NOT US?

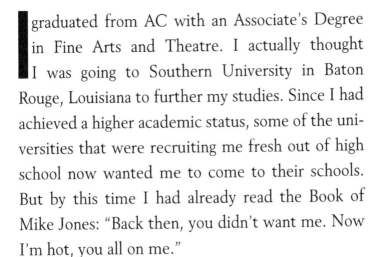

graduated from AC with an Associate's Degree in Fine Arts and Theatre. I actually thought I was going to Southern University in Baton Rouge, Louisiana to further my studies. Since I had achieved a higher academic status, some of the universities that were recruiting me fresh out of high school now wanted me to come to their schools. But by this time I had already read the Book of Mike Jones: "Back then, you didn't want me. Now I'm hot, you all on me."

I wanted to go to Southern University for two reasons. One, I had learned a little bit about historically black colleges (HBCUs) and I wanted to attend one. And two, I was dating a girl I thought I was going to marry, and she was attending Southern. I wanted to be there next to my Boo, so we could be like Dwayne Wayne and Whitley on "A Different World". My parents told me if I came back to Houston and attended Texas Southern University they would help me get a car. Immediately I realized I could get another Boo.

I decided to go to Texas Southern University (TSU). These were some of the best years of my life. If I could clone my college career and sell it, some kid would love me. Outside of getting an awesome education, great experiences and meeting some amazing people, some of whom I am still friends with today, the biggest thing about TSU for me was it was a slice of life. It taught me if I could make it there, I could make it anywhere. HBCUs should give you an honorary master's degree when you earn your bachelor's.

It's not the work at TSU that makes it hard to graduate; it's all the distractions around the work. There was a DJ on the yard every day. As you were walking to class, he was playing all of the latest and hottest jams. It tempted you and make you ask, "Do I really need to go to class today?"

Of course I needed to go to class, but at that moment the yard was hot. The girls were wearing their daisy dukes, and I just wanted to be a part of it. Therefore, I had to structure and organize my schedule to accommodate my desire to be on the yard.

I had no problem waking up early because I was used to doing it every Sunday for church. The yard didn't usually get kicking until about 11 a.m. and lasted until 2 p.m. So, I scheduled all of my classes from 8 a.m. to 11 a.m., Monday through Friday. At 11 a.m., I was posted up on the yard ready to do my thing.

The summer before my last year of college, I stayed at my parents' house for a few weeks. During school, I lived in the dorms; no curfew, no questions, etc. Life was good. However, when I came home for the summer, I had a 1 a.m. curfew. I didn't even leave the house until 11 p.m. and my mother wanted to know the who, what and where about everything!

I had been missing curfews and getting into trouble with my parents, so I talked to my dad about me being grown and still being treated like a child and he said, "This house has two adults, not three." He was basically saying, if you are grown, move out on your own.

So, I went and got my own apartment. My mother begged me not to go out into the world on my own so soon, but I didn't listen. She even cried when I packed my stuff and put it into the car they were paying for.

I asked them if I could take my bedroom set and they said, "No, you're grown, so get your own". My parents didn't buy anything for my little, old apartment. It got real for me real quick! I'd never paid bills before, grocery shopped or cooked for myself.

I would sneak over to my parents' house when they were at work and wash and dry my clothes, then grocery shop their through their food like I was at Walmart. All of the luxuries I used to have living with them, like Tabasco sauce, microwave popcorn, eggs, milk and cereal had disappeared and I had to fend for myself.

One day, I went to my parents' house when I knew they were at work, only to find that they had changed the locks on the door! At first, I thought I was at the wrong house. I wiggled the key over and over again to no avail. To make matters worse, I had a young lady from the college with me.

I went to the neighbor's house to call my mom. I asked her if they changed the locks and she said, "Yes, we were tired of you stealing from us."

I was 22 years old at that time. I had my parents' prayers, but I was no longer in their pockets. I grew up that day and realized "grown" is when you're on your own and don't need a loan.

During my college career, I met these six guys who were majoring in my field of Radio, TV and Film. They were John Tucker, Chris Mayberry, Christopher Holt, John Jones, Cliff McBean, and Kehlin Farooq. We didn't grow up together, but we all wanted to excel in the entertainment field.

We created a frat-like clique called *Why Not Us?* and started making short films. We felt like, why not us? Why can't we have success fame, money and the things we want now?

We started making these films around campus. At first, people were making fun of us, calling us fake Spike Lees and things like that, but after our films became popular, everybody wanted to be a part of them. All of the girls wanted to be in our short films, and they would hang our movie posters on their dorm room walls.

We went from campus famous to city famous. Local networks interviewed us, exposing our talent. That caused our group to grow into a company.

We got a DBA for our name, established a bank account, business cards and once again, it was on! Companies would call us to do local commercials for television and radio. We did music videos, wrote treatments, and directed and produced videos for local artists. We became so popular; we would get featured on the local TV stations and in newspaper articles and were sought out to promote shows and write radio commercials for prominent clientele.

When I was about to graduate from TSU with a GPA of 3.6, and I remembered we had to take an exit exam. I never understood why you had to take an exit exam if you had taken all the courses. So, now I had to prove that I qualified to graduate.

Another test? I was definitely nervous about taking another test that had such an effect on my future. However, this one was different! I knew this material, or let me say it like this: I should know it. It's all the things I should have learned in the school of communications.

When you take the exit exam, they used to post the results by your social security number. There were three possible outcomes for the test results: passed, barely passed and fail.

I took the exit exam and went to see the results. I looked for my social security number under *"Passed"* and I didn't see it. I looked under *"Barely Passed"* and low and behold, there it was. I was so excited. The chairman of the Communications Department was like, "What are you so happy for?"

I told him, "I passed the exit exam."

And he said, "Yeah, but you barely passed."

I asked him, "Do I still get to graduate?"

He said, "Yes."

I reiterated, "Well, I passed!"

That's just like getting to Heaven. Nobody cares that you barely made it, as long as you get to get in and tell your story of how you made it over. I realized at that moment, folks will always try to belittle you. A pass is a pass in my book.

Putting "barely passed" next to my social security number did not affect my self-esteem at all. I walked across the stage and graduated from Texas Southern University proudly!

ERICA

After I graduated from TSU, I immediately went from the graduation line to the unemployment line. School had me fooled. I thought when you graduated from college; businesses and companies would be waiting on the other side of the stage just ready to be handing out big money jobs.

I didn't realize that once I graduated, I had to continue working to try and get where I was going in life. I was sold the idea that school was the end all to be all. This definitely wasn't so. I must admit it was discouraging. One thing I learned from my biological father that stuck with me in this situation was to never quit and always finish what you start.

When I was playing Pop Warner Football, I was quarterback. I was good, but my offensive line was horrible. I kept getting sacked. I came to the sideline, threw my helmet down, and said, "I quit!"

My dad came from the stands and told me to pick up my helmet and get back in the game. He said if I quit, I would think it's okay to quit every time something was hard or difficult.

Even though I didn't want to go to school, I thought not going would be the equivalent of quitting. In light of this, I ended up going to grad school. I didn't really want to go back to school, but I went to graduate school by default. I was a graduate assistant coach for the women's volleyball and basketball teams. This is how I was able to pay for school.

My good friend, Dr. Dwalah Fisher, was the volleyball head coach. She paid all my tuition from my second year at TSU all the way through grad school. When you have complete confidence in God, He ALWAYS comes through.

Psalms 46:1 *God is our refuge and strength, a very present help in trouble.*

It's important to pay attention and remember His plan is so much sweeter than ours. I met Dwalah at Willowridge High School. She was a star volleyball athlete with bad knees. I would work with her from time to time during her rehab. She appreciated me so much; she paid my way through grad school. Look at God!

Philippians 4:19: *But my God shall supply all your need according to his riches in glory by Christ Jesus.*

I was in grad school, and really not enjoying where I was in life. I mean, I was having fun, and I was not depressed, because that's never me. I was disappointed because I thought when I graduated, I would have more things going on.

One evening, I was sitting on The Yard talking to my friend, and that's when I saw her. It was love at first sight — literally. My "wife-to-be" walked by, and it seemed like the sun was shining right on her.

That first time I saw her, she looked like her name was Mrs. Marcus D. Wiley. She walked like a lady. She had the kind of smile that lights up a room, and her lip gloss was poppin'.

I stepped to her a couple of days later in the cafeteria. I walked up to her and asked her a string of questions: "Are you married? Are you engaged? Do you have more than two kids? Do you have a terrible disease?"

She said "no" to all of them and then asked me why all the questions. I told her, "I'm just trying to see what's going stop us from being together."

We met on December 12, 1996, were engaged by April 11, 1997, and got married on August 23, 1997. The reason we got married so fast is because she was going to have to go to Dallas for the summer, and I felt like if we didn't do it then, we were not going to do it.

We ended up having to shack up. That's right, the preacher's son was shacking up. I remember my mom and dad hated the fact that we were living together. We had to save our money and get everything together so we could have a quick wedding. It wasn't because she was pregnant, like some people might have thought. It was just that I was tired of seeing the disappointment and shame on my parents' faces.

Love was in the air, but there was definitely a catch. I told my wife I had dreams before I met her, and I needed her to hold me down for five years while I chased those dreams. I told her there were things I wanted to be in life. I just believe that until a man is happy with his situation, it's going to be impossible for him to be effective, efficient and empowering to his family.

Many guys don't like where they are in life, so when they just get a job to support the family they remain unfulfilled. Employment is a good thing, but it's only when doing something that you really love are you able to have passion and purpose with your position.

At that time, my wife was young and completely in love with me. She told me she had been praying for a good "dude" to come along. She was so into me then that I could have told her the sky was purple and she would have never looked up to check. She would've just believed me!

Now, she will definitely look up and say, "Stop lying so much" But because she believed in me back then, it made me want to make it happen. Quitting, in this case, would be letting two people down and I couldn't let that happen.

So, I needed my wife to keep a job while I chased my dream. My wife didn't have a problem with doing this. However, holding me down meant no grumbling. No mumbling. No complaining. No smart comments like, "You ain't found a job yet?" No attitude. No talking under her breath, while still giving me as much nasty as I can handle.

I promised her that if after five years, nothing happened for me, if it didn't pop off, I would get a job. My wife agreed to do this because she knew I had potential; but, I know potential is overrated. I tell people all the time, don't fall in love with somebody's potential.

A woman that wears a size 22 dress has the potential to wear a size 2. But, will she ever reach her full potential? Probably not. So, it's important to love the 22 whether it becomes a 2 or not.

My wife bought into Marcus D. Wiley, the guy who was in between jobs. That's who she fell in love with, and I believe if I had been in between jobs for the rest of my life, she would still love me. But thank God, I'm not.

FACT #2

"WHAT ABOUT YOUR FRIENDS?"

Mark 2:1-5

And again he entered into Capernaum after some days; and it was noised that he was in the house. And straightway many were gathered together, insomuch that there was no room to receive them, no, not so much as about the door: and he preached the word unto them. And they come unto him, bringing one sick of the palsy, which was borne of four. And when they could not come nigh unto him for the press, they uncovered the roof where he was: and when they had broken it up, they let down the bed wherein the sick of the palsy lay. When Jesus saw their faith, he said unto the sick of the palsy, Son, thy sins be forgiven thee.

The question is have you done all you can do?

I know you have done what you were supposed to do — a few things here and there.

You may have even tried some things, but have you done all you can do?

In this story four friends believed if they could get their paralytic partner to Jesus, He would heal him. So they packed him up, picked him up and carried him to where Jesus was.

However, when they got there they were faced with a roadblock. The church was packed! It was sold out! Three was no room and all the entrances are crowded.

It's good to have friends with faith and hustle because I can hear them saying, "Nobody told us the road would be easy, but I don't believe God has brought us this far just to leave us."

They could have given up and said, "I guess it's not meant to be" or "It must not be in God's will." Instead, they got creative and showed God how badly they wanted this.

So they climbed up on the roof, carrying a man who couldn't climb for himself.

What about your friends? The people you spend all or most of your time with? I know they're down with you, but will they climb for you?

Because this mission called for more than just faith in God, it required faith and hustle!

So, when you run into the crowds in life, and you're faced with the climb of life and find yourself on the roof of life, do like the friends in this story and tear the roof off!

To me, the roof symbolizes your mind! Don't box your thoughts in. Get creative — explore all the possibilities. Don't limit yourself. Because when God is in it, there are no limits!

WILEYWOOD

Normally, five years is a long time. But when you give yourself a certain amount of time to find your purpose, to find your passion and to find your position in life, it goes by pretty quick. For me in this case, five years literally felt like five minutes.

In the five-year span my wife allowed me for chasing my dreams, I was a bank teller, a high school teacher, a middle school teacher, a volleyball and basketball coach, a college recruiter and a producer of a show called "Hits from the Streets" on BET (Black Entertainment Television).

Hits from the Streets was a video show where we played pranks on people from the streets. "Why Not Us/Why Not Now" Productions from college paid off. John Tucker sent a movie that we did to BET and they offered him an editor's position.

Within a few months he moved to the producer of a show called, Teen Summit. A few months later, he became producer of another show called, Rap City. John had "the juice," and he was able to help five of us secure employment at BET.

Hits from the Streets was a good show, and I had the opportunity to meet a bunch of people in the entertainment industry. I also was afforded the opportunity to learn the business of entertainment: how to travel, how to survive on the road, and how to manage people with difficult personalities.

While at BET, I thought I was going to end up getting my own show. That was my goal. We put together a lot of pilots, and these pilots never got picked up. However, I would see our ideas on other shows, meaning I never got picked up, but our ideas did. If you catch my drift...

I was working for the industry, but the industry wasn't working for me. I'd go to all of the industry parties, mixers and socials — meeting a lot of people and passing out business cards — but to no avail. It was all smoke and mirrors. It was during this time at BET that I discovered I had faith, but I didn't have hustle. I was doing just enough to get by. Just enough to say I'd tried.

I remember one day I was at ESPN Zone, an eatery in Downtown DC when I saw a young guy with dreads, wearing a nice tailored suit, sitting at the bar and working on some type of beat machine. I asked him what was he doing, and he said he was working on music. I asked if he was a producer, and he said, "No, I'm a lawyer; but, I want to be a music producer."

This puzzled me. I thought, *Why would a lawyer want to be a music producer?* He looked pretty cool. His suit fit, so I'm pretty sure he made good money. He had on a nice pair of Bruno Mali shoes, too. Why would someone waste all that time in law school and then want to do something else?

It was at that moment that something clicked inside of me. I realized I wasn't living up to my full potential. It wasn't that I was lazy; I just didn't know that I could do more. All this time, I thought you were only supposed to do one thing. This young man opened my eyes and made me want to be more and do more.

I compare it to the Garden of Eden in the Bible. The garden had four streams running through it. Many people equate this to having four streams of income. I realized I could do more than just one thing, and I am more than what I have already become. I began to think about what else this life had in store for me. The lid of my mind had been opened.

So, I took a trip to L.A. to try and find out exactly how this industry works. I had an opportunity to visit FOX studios, and I met with Mitsy Wilson. She was the senior vice president of diversity, and her job was to put people of color in front of the camera as well as behind the camera in roles like, writers, directors and producers.

We sat and talked and then we walked to her office. On a table in her office were scripts, VHS and beta tapes stacked from the table to the ceiling. These submissions were from people who were trying to break into the entertainment business. I asked her if she had to read through all of that, and she said, "No." She would not be going through *any* of it.

I assumed she would be passing this assignment to her interns, but she quickly corrected me and said the only thing her interns were going to do is return everything to the senders. She went on to say, "The sad part about this is the next Denzel Washington, Halle Berry and Spike Lee could be in this stack, but we'll never know."

So then I asked her, "If you don't look at these things, how does one get discovered?" And that's when she blew me away.

She said, "If you're going to get into this business, you're going to have to come to us by way of recommendation. The only way we look at tapes is if an established person like Will Smith comes in and says, 'Take a look at this person' or 'Take a look at this script,' or 'Take a look at this idea.' Then we will consider it."

In a nutshell, she was saying if you're going to break into this business, you're going to have to create your own buzz so that Hollywood will come knocking at your door.

At that moment, I knew I had to make my own noise. That's when I came up with Wileywood Entertainment. It is my own brand of entertainment, where I make people laugh and think at the same time. My goal was to be a service for you and to you. It was right then in that moment in her office that I gave birth to Wileywood. *I didn't even know I was pregnant!*

CHAPTER 8

SHOW ME THE MONEY

My five years hurried to a close, as the pastors would say. My wife did her part. She didn't fuss, complain, or whine not one time about me chasing my dreams.

Now it was time for me to do my part and get a divorce. Not from her, but from my dreams. After all, I did promise that if I didn't get it in five years, I would come home and get a good job, be a good husband and live the good life...blah, blah, blah.

I prayed to God and asked Him to just put me somewhere He wanted me to serve and work, so I told Him I'd start at the bottom and work my way up to the top.

I landed a job working at a church as the Director of Events. I really enjoyed my job, but the pay sucked and there were too many politics in ministry. I didn't like that I couldn't be myself.

For example, I would come to work and people would ask, "How you're doing?"

People would respond with all these lies like, "I'm too blessed to be stressed," "I'm too anointed to be disappointed," and "I'm blessed and highly favored."

This frustrated me, because I wanted to come to work and just tell the truth. When asked how I felt, I wanted to say, "I feel horrible, my wife and I are not getting along, my car keeps breaking down and I don't feel blessed, I feel cursed!" I guess I really didn't enjoy working at the church, per se. I loved the people, but I didn't enjoy working at the church house.

I don't always say and do the right things, at least according to church folk. I have a mind of my own and a lot of times in church that is unacceptable. I also wasn't a good yes-man.

At this particular church, you had to be a good yes-man. For some reason it made the pastor feel good about himself having a yes-man around him, but I was way too intelligent to play dumb. Despite my frustrations, I felt like the Lord had put me there, so I was going to stick with it. But, God had other plans for me.

During my tenure at the church, I became a college professor at Texas Southern University. I always wanted to teach on the collegiate level. After my experiences as a middle and high school teacher, I felt I would be better suited teaching college students.

I had a teacher in college named Dr. Ronald Lomas. He was the man! All the girls wanted him, and all the guys wanted to be like him. He had an answer for everything. He had a unique way of making difficult things seem so plain and simple.

Dr. Lomas really inspired me, and sparked a desire in me to teach. I wanted to be able to inspire students who came from dysfunctional backgrounds, assuring them they could make it and be successful in life.

At HBCUs you have a lot of inner city kids who think that they won't go far in life because of their upbringing, surroundings and test scores. I wanted to tell them that they could go farther than their expectations and they could make it.

I had no idea I would be teaching so soon. I thought I'd come back to teach as an old man after I retired from my bright and brilliant acting career, but I came back a whole lot sooner. I must admit, I really enjoyed teaching. Still to this day, it's a blessing to see the light bulb come on in a youngster's mind and knowing that they *get it* now.

I was doing my thing working on staff at the church, and I was also teaching at TSU. Things were going pretty good, but I wasn't making enough money. My wife and I were robbing Peter to pay Paul, and I'm not talking about the ones in the Bible. It was crazy, because I was having trouble keeping the lights on in the house, but all the lights on my dashboard in the car were always on — gas light, oil light, engine light, water light and every light possible. I started to park the car in the house so we could have lights.

I was up for an evaluation at the church. The pastor and I had already talked about a number that he was going to put me at before my evaluation. At that time, I was making $28,000, and the pastor said that he was going to bump me up to at least $42,000.

We talked about my financial situation and my educational background. I had three degrees, plus it was noted that I was doing an exceptional job in my current position. I thought my experience, performance, education and friendship would be honored, but this wasn't the case.

I was in the evaluation meeting with the 'powers that be', and all of a sudden, I'm quoted a salary that was significantly lower than what was originally discussed. It was almost like a movie. It was documented that I would be making $52,000.

I was like, "Okay, cool! I'm going from $28,000 to $52,000." I'm on the cusp of giving God all the praise and letting everybody know He's worthy! All of a sudden, the pastor walks in, looks at the amount written on the dry erase board and says, he's not going to be able to pay that amount. He says that he will only be able to pay $34,000.

Now, when he and I talked, it was $42,000. I get in the meeting, and it's $52,000. And now it's down to $34,000. Imagine the emotions that were raging inside of me. To top it off, he tells me to go and pray about this number with my wife.

I told him, "There are some things God don't even want you to pray about, and this is one of them!" I called my wife and told her to email me over a two weeks notice letter.

We were doing pretty badly financially. The guys on staff kept telling me not to make a rash decision, and just to pray about it; but, my mind was made up. I was outta there! God knew that I would never leave that job if things were good, so I believe He had to frustrate the situation in order for me to get where He wanted me to be.

Even now, when people tell me they've lost their job or they got fired, I always tell them that getting let go is sometimes a promotion. You know we can't see it every time, but sometimes the only way that God is going to remove us from one place and take us to another is by frustrating the situation and making us uncomfortable. If He didn't frustrate me while I was working on staff at the church, I would've never left.

Keep reading. Trust me, I understood everything better, once I left.

CHAPTER 9

ALL GOD SAYS I AM

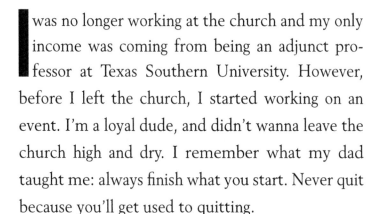

I was no longer working at the church and my only income was coming from being an adjunct professor at Texas Southern University. However, before I left the church, I started working on an event. I'm a loyal dude, and didn't wanna leave the church high and dry. I remember what my dad taught me: always finish what you start. Never quit because you'll get used to quitting.

Turns out this event would be the event to get the old entertainment ball back rolling. I was the host of the event, doing what I typically did on stage: making people laugh.

I hosted all the church events. Churches use their members to do something for free that professionals get paid for and call it your "reasonable service."

A few days later, a lady who attended the event called the church wanting to talk to the comedian who hosted the show. The receptionist told her that I no longer worked there, but she gave her my cell phone number. (Footnote: It's good to treat people right.) Had I left the church on postal terms, they could have very well tried to block that blessing, but because I left in good standing, they did not.

So, the lady called me and asked me to do comedy at her coffee shop for their one year anniversary. I told her I was not a comedian, but she was like, "You're very funny!"

I said, "Thank you, but that was in front of my church — people I know personally and am familiar with."

She said, "Oh ,well. I was going to pay you $500 to do the show."

I replied, "What's that date again?"

The lady thought I was a comedian. She literally saw a comedian in me before I actually became one professionally. The first time I told her I wasn't a comedian, she could've said, "Okay, bye." But she was persistent and kept making mention of how funny I was. Here was God giving me a hint, sending me a raft, throwing me a bone and I was steadily talking about what I'm not. God was telling me, "I know you're not, but I AM!

September 20, 2002 came around and I had no idea how my comedic debut would go. I didn't even know how to put a joke together. Thanks to AC, I did have structure, organization and presentation; plus, I needed that $500. I did the show, and it went very well. I was so thankful for the people that laughed even when the jokes weren't that funny; they definitely encouraged me.

Three days later, the owner of the coffee house said she wanted to do a show once a month, and she would pay me $750. I was like, "Huh? What? Okaaaay!!! Let me get this straight. You're going to pay me, $750 for one hour."

She said, "Yes."

I was like *Wow. Look at God!*

When God shows you a glimpse of your future, that's not the time to sit back and watch Him work. That's the time for you to get up off your blessed assurance and hustle — because God is not going to do what you *won't* do; He's *gone* do what you *can't* do.

Wow! Who would've thought I would be a full-time, working comedian. I am going all over the country doing shows. I'm on what they call the chitlin' circuit. I'm doing small clubs, churches, talent shows, bar mitzvahs, wedding receptions and even funerals. I'm killing it. Things are looking good for me.

I started out driving to shows, staying in motels and getting checks with instructions. Then I progressed to flying to shows, staying in five star hotels and getting good checks in advance.

People began to tell me I should quit teaching because comedy was going so well. I later found out that comedians didn't consider me a full-time comedian or a true comedian because I had another job. They literally wanted me to quit my fa'sho money so I'd be broke like them, taking anything somebody would offer me to perform; casting my pearls to swine.

> Matthew 7:6: *Give not that which is holy unto the dogs, neither cast ye your pearls before swine, lest they trample them under their feet, and turn again and rend you.*

Ironically, all the comedians I look up to have more than one job. Steve Harvey, for example, is a comedian, radio host, TV Talk Show Host, TV Game Show Host, author, actor, clothing line designer, and movie producer. The same thing with Kevin Hart, Rickey Smiley, and Jamie Foxx.

I now knew where I was trying to go required me to have more than one job. Plus, I can do more than one thing. As a matter of fact, I can do *all things*.

> Philippians 4:13: *I can do all things through Christ which strengtheneth me.*

Around this time, I opened up for some major entertainers. The list is too long to name, plus I'm getting charged by the letter to print this. My first comedy tour was with a guy named Duval Murchinson out of Lansing, Michigan called Laugh-a-lujah. It featured comedians Rod-Z out of Orlando, Darrian Perkins and Vyck Cooly out of Atlanta, Georgia and Yours Truly.

After that tour, I did The Rickey Smiley and Friends Tour. The friends changed from night to night, but I was a mainstay. I was beasting! I was hungry, raw, fresh and I left the stage every night to a standing ovation.

What I did not know was that I was doing too much. In the comedy game, it's not proper to outshine or make it hard for the headliner. I was in no way trying to outdo Rickey Smiley. I was well aware whose name was on the marquee. I was well aware whose name sold the tickets, and

I was well aware who the people came out to see. I just looked at it as an opportunity for me to get recognized.

I was the feature act before the headliner. I had a 30-minute set. I never went over my time, but I remember them reducing it to 20 minutes, then to 15 minutes, then to 10 minutes.

What they were basically telling me without telling me was that I was doing too much. But I didn't know better. I was new to the game, and I was just trying to make a name for myself.

Now that I'm a headliner, I better understand the comedy game's perspectives, but I still let the young comics do their thing. It doesn't faze me, because again I'm well aware of whose name is on the marquee. I am well aware of whose name is selling the tickets, and I'm well aware of who the people are coming to see.

FACT #3

"SAVED, TALENTED, AND LAZY"

Matthew 25:14-30:

14For the kingdom of heaven is as a man travelling into a far country, who called his own servants, and delivered unto them his goods.

15And unto one he gave five talents, to another two, and to another one; to every man according to his several ability; and straightway took his journey.

16Then he that had received the five talents went and traded with the same, and made them other five talents.

17And likewise he that had received two, he also gained other two.

18But he that had received one went and digged in the earth, and hid his lord's money.

19After a long time the lord of those servants cometh, and reckoneth with them.

²⁰And so he that had received five talents came and brought other five talents, saying, Lord, thou deliveredst unto me five talents: behold, I have gained beside them five talents more.

²¹His lord said unto him, Well done, thou good and faithful servant: thou hast been faithful over a few things, I will make thee ruler over many things: enter thou into the joy of thy lord.

²²He also that had received two talents came and said, Lord, thou delivered st unto me two talents: behold, I have gained two other talents beside them.

²³His lord said unto him, Well done, good and faithful servant; thou hast been faithful over a few things, I will make thee ruler over many things: enter thou into the joy of thy lord.

²⁴Then he which had received the one talent came and said, Lord, I knew thee that thou art an hard man, reaping where thou hast not sown, and gathering where thou hast not strawed:

²⁵And I was afraid, and went and hid thy talent in the earth: lo, there thou hast that is thine.

²⁶His lord answered and said unto him, Thou wicked and slothful servant, thou knewest that I reap where I sowed not, and gather where I have not strawed:

²⁷Thou oughtest therefore to have put my money to the exchangers, and then at my coming I should have received mine own with usury.

²⁸Take therefore the talent from him, and give it unto him which hath ten talents.

²⁹For unto every one that hath shall be given, and he shall have abundance: but from him that hath not shall be taken away even that which he hath.

³⁰And cast ye the unprofitable servant into outer darkness: there shall be weeping and gnashing of teeth.

In this very familiar parable my thesis is once again proven when I say God honors your faith and rewards your hustle. There are a lot of talented individuals who are doing nothing with their talent. They talk about those who are less talented. They say things like "they can't sing, they're not funny, I'm better than them."

They also talk about what they would not do. Stuff like, "I would not drive three or four hours to perform. I won't fly coach. I won't work for that amount of money."

I like to call them saved, talented, and lazy!

What I get out of this parable is, at some point God is gonna pay your situation a visit.

Those who believe in God, He is gonna make a cameo appearance in your circumstance. And when He does, He's gonna ask you, "What have you been doing with what I gave you? Besides running your mouth, what have you been doing with your skills, gifts and talents?"

If you have been sitting on your blessed assurance waiting on God to do something you could have been doing, you're probably gonna get called out of your name! I believe wicked and lazy were the names used in the parable.

I used to say, "What God has for you is for you," when I would hear people say things like, "They got my job" or "I should have that position."

But after reading this parable, they might be right. God may have taken your job, your position and given it to somebody who may be less talented, but more faithful, have more hustle, and be more trustworthy and dependable.

Matthews 25:29: *For unto every one that hath shall be given, and he shall have abundance: but from him that hath not shall be taken away even that which he hath.*

CHAPTER 10

THE POINT OF IT ALL

As my career was blowin' up, so was my marriage. Professionally, I was getting better. Personally, I was getting worse. I was spending a lot of time on the road because I was in hustle mode. My wife was at home. She didn't have a problem with me being on the road, because it was providing a good living for us.

I believe my wife began to feel inadequate — like she didn't matter as much anymore. For five years, she carried me. She had the good job. She made the money, which made her the centerpiece of our relationship.

We talked about everything — every decision — because she had the money. I had to talk to her about spending her money. But, when I became the breadwinner and didn't need her money any longer, this caused problems and insecurities in our marriage.

My gift to my wife, for holding me down for five years, was that she would never have to pay or worry about a bill for the rest of her life. Now that don't mean she don't have to work, because a woman who don't work is unattractive to ME!

However, now my wife goes to work and can spend her money on whatever she wants to spend it on. Hair, nails, beat face, clothes, food, travel, shopping, etc., etc. From the outside looking in, we are living the good life. But from the inside, things have changed, and we didn't have the capacity for the adjustment. We were in uncharted territory.

We ended up getting separated for six months. During the time of separation, I was cool with it at first. I didn't want any more responsibility. We didn't own anything and we didn't have any children, so the split wasn't messy. I gave her everything in the house. I figured I could start over from scratch because I was making money now, plus I could put all of my energy into my career.

I went out on a few dates with some pretty nice ladies, but they all had the same problem. They did not know me. They didn't know my story. They weren't with me when I had nothing. They were coming in at the top and didn't start with me from the bottom.

Around the fifth month of the separation, I was being honored on Bobby Jones' Gospel Special on BET. I was highlighted as one of the five top clean comics in the country, which was big because it was on television!

This really fueled my career by placing me center stage in the faith community. Churches from all over the country begin to call me to come perform.

The night of the Bobby Jones taping was a huge success. It was packed. I did my thing, and when I got off stage, the first person I wanted to call to say, "Hey, we made it!" was my wife. But, we were separated and hadn't been talking to each other.

I wanted to call her and say, "I told you. Stick with me! We're going places!" But she wasn't with me.

Here I am, in Miami, where I'm supposed to be living la vida loca. I'm on South Beach, staying at a five-star hotel. Half-naked mamas are everywhere, but I was miserable. I just hit a major milestone in my life, and the person I'm supposed to be sharing it with ain't here. What was all the hustling for? Success without substance is insignificant. I mean, what's the point?

As I'm flying home from Miami to Houston, I fall asleep on the plane and God starts talking to me. God usually talks to me on the plane. I don't know why; maybe because I'm closer to Him at the time.

He said, "So, let me get this straight. You're going to divorce her because she does some things you don't like, but I haven't divorced you and you do a *whole lot of things* I don't like. Not only have I not divorced you, I have not even exposed you."

Wow. He was right. It's crazy how we'll hustle for a career but won't hustle to keep our marriage.

Plus, I didn't want to be the guy who had the chick that was with him when he didn't have anything, and as soon as he gets something, he leaves her.

I know people grow, and I know people change; but, I wanted to grow and change with Erica. So, I went to her apartment and told her, "God has spoken. Let the church say, 'Amen!'" Seventeen years later we're still here.

CHAPTER 11

HUSTLE HIGHLIGHTS & HARDSHIPS

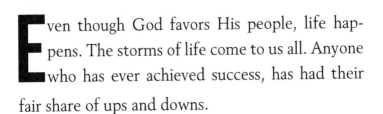

E ven though God favors His people, life happens. The storms of life come to us all. Anyone who has ever achieved success, has had their fair share of ups and downs.

I remember my mom telling me her best friend, Edna Harris' son, Marlon, bought her a house, and she was bragging on how good he takes care of his mother. I always wanted to buy my parents a house. I knew with me being the only child, someday, I would have to take care of my parents. Neither one of my parents had a retirement plan which meant I was the plan.

Though I wasn't a professional athlete or a superstar, comedy was taking good care of me! For the first time in my life I had money in the bank. I had a checking and savings account.

I decided I needed to let people know I make money, so I went to the Mercedes Benz dealership to buy a luxury car — not for me, but for the sake of status. I test drove it! The seats embraced me. The color looked good on me. I found out it's true what they say, "luxury is the only way to go," but right before I signed my name on the dotted line, conviction kicked in.

My mother had been telling me that our old neighborhood in "Mo City" was getting like 4th Ward. Crime was on the rise, the neighborhood was on the decline and she'd been hearing gun shots. Plus, she mentioned she needed health insurance.

All of this was going through my mind just as I was about to sign for my new car. When I told the salesman that I wasn't gonna get the car, he told me that I just had a case of cold feet. It wasn't cold feet it was conviction!

Now how would I look, driving around in a Benz when my momma can't afford to get a check up? So instead of buying a Benz, on August 26, 2005 I bought my parents a house! It was one of the greatest days of my life.

November 12, 2007 was another great day! That's the day my son, Chase Jaxon Wiley, was born. Believe it or not, I had a show that night, and according to my business manager, Neal, my performance was all over the place. I kept looking at him because he would give me the signal that we had to go because Erica is about to go into labor.

About 25 minutes into my routine, he gave me the 'wrap it up' sign and I told the crowd I had to go. We sped down the highway to the hospital. I ran in and they put me in some scrubs and took me in the delivery room. There was my wife — all drugged up!

Doctor Hare asked me was I ready because the baby was ready! I grabbed the camcorder and filmed one of the best horror films I have ever seen in my life!

I was so proud of my wife for getting through it, and I was extremely happy for her because she wanted a baby. God keeps showing up!

Chase is seven now and prays every night for a little sister. Kids! Having Chase has made me hustle even more. Kids are expensive! However, he is not a burden, he is a blessing!

One of the worst days of my life was when the IRS took all of the money out of my account without any warning. The people who prepared my taxes were foul, incompetent and negligent. Because of their lack of integrity, I got caught in the crossfire and was wiped out!

I was sick! This wasn't dope money, this was joke money! I earned it! I worked hard for it and they took all of it! To my knowledge, I didn't do anything wrong, but the people who prepared my taxes were dead wrong! I had just started making money and all of a sudden I owed the IRS six figures!

When the teller at the bank turned the monitor around and showed me a remaining balance of $43.26 in my account, I almost passed out. However, I kept my composure, walked to my truck, sat down and began to pray.

I said, "God, thank you for allowing me the opportunity to make money. Though I didn't do anything wrong, I am liable. I refuse to trip over this because I know you will help me take back all the devil has stolen from me and help me to recover all. I don't worship money, I worship you and you know I have a family to support so I thank you in advance for restoration!"

It was a tough day but I made it through it and God hasn't failed me yet!

Another tough day was December 21, 2009. This was the day God called Joe home. When he was pronounced dead in the hospital, I stood over him and thanked him for taking care of my mother and me. I also told him "I got it from here."

As I told you, I knew I would have to eventually take care of my parents. When he died, I felt like he was passing the mantle to me. I am grateful for Joe. He was a good husband and father. He came in my life at the right time and took care of us when we needed it! Rest in Heaven, Joe Culton!

CHAPTER 12

CAN YOU HEAR ME NOW?

T hough I was touring the country doing comedy and working at the university teaching, I realized in order to ascend in the industry, I needed another job. There were rumors that a Praise FM Radio Gospel Station was coming to Houston. It would be Houston's first 24-hour Inspiration Station.

I immediately started working on my air check (radio jargon for demo tape). I created this show for the radio called, "The Sunday After Church Drive with Marcus D. Wiley." It was going to be from 2 p.m. to 6 p.m. My air check consisted of a bunch of funny bits, including trademark characters and quips like "Bishop Secular."

I took my air check to Praise Houston's radio station, but the program director gingerly cast it aside without even listening to it.

"Do you have any experience?" she asked with unconvincing interest.

I told her I worked at a radio station in college.

She pretended to probe. "How long ago was that?"

"About ten years ago," I smiled.

"Radio's changed," she noted, and quickly added that I was "eons behind." She finished with, "We're not hiring."

A new station not hiring? Yeah, right. I wasn't mad that I didn't get the job. I wasn't mad that she talked greasy and fly to me. I was mad that she didn't listen to what I'd prepared. All my hard work was going unnoticed.

> Hebrews 6:10: *And without faith it is impossible to please God, because anyone who comes to Him must*

believe that He exists and that he rewards those who earnestly seek Him.

I received a phone call to host a show for the Houston Black Chamber of Commerce. I remember it being very bourgeois. The audience was stiff, stuck-up, uppity — kinda like an 8 o'clock church service. However, they were honoring five-time Grammy award winning gospel artist, Yolanda Adams.

As I was going through my routine, it seemed as if only Yolanda Adams and her table were laughing. Don't get me wrong, other people were laughing, but Yolanda was laughing like Richard Pryor was on the stage. She was loud, bending over and slapping the table. It was like I paid her to laugh.

Even though the rest of the room was starch, she and her guests really enjoyed themselves. When the show was over and we were at the valet getting our vehicles, and I told her it was nice to meet her. She said, "Same, to you. You were *really funny!*"

About two months later, who knew Yolanda Adams would have her own local radio show on Praise Houston called the "Yolanda Adams Morning Show." She hit the airwaves with one of Houston's legendary radio personalities, Funky Larry Jones, who later changed his name to Brother Larry for the Gospel station. There was also supposed to be a comedian on the show with them, but I later found out that there were contract disputes and they could not agree. I like to say, *God blocked it*!

So, they opened up auditions for a few hand-picked comedians. The radio station had a select group of comedians they wanted to bring in with whom they were familiar. However, Yolanda said she'd just seen a comedian a couple of months ago who was hilarious. She couldn't remember my full name, but she said, "I believe his last name was Wiley."

Funky Larry Jones knew me because he hosted a couple of shows I'd performed on. So he said, "You're talking about Marcus D. Wiley." Larry had my number in his phone and they called me one morning around 6 a.m.

I thought it was a joke because I have the type of friends who would call joking with me that early in the morning.

> The Bible says, in Proverbs 18:16: *A man's gift maketh room for him, and bringeth him before great men.*

Although I had only spoken to her from in passing, Yolanda talked to me as if we'd been relatives all my life. We later found out we *are* related, my grandmother and her grandfather are siblings. It was so casual, that the magnitude of the moment seemed surreal. She asked me if I'd like to audition to be on her new radio show.

After I'd gathered myself and realized it wasn't a joke, I said, "Yes, I would love to!"

I went to the station that first Friday, suited and booted. Hair cut, smelling good and Carmex on my lips. Although people in radio land couldn't see me, Yolanda could. We had a good time, so they invited me back the next Friday. Once again, I was suited and booted. Hair cut, smelling good and Carmex on my lips. Although people in radio land couldn't see me, Yolanda could. We had a better time, so I got invited back for the next Friday.

I didn't break the mold. I was suited and booted. Hair cut, smelling good and Carmex on my lips. Although people in radio land couldn't see me, Yolanda could. Presentation is everything.

We had an awesome time, and that's when Yolanda leaned back and said the sweetest words I'd heard since my wife said, "I do," —"You've got the job."

YES!!!!!!!!!!!!! Three jobs! I am a college professor, a standup comedian, and now I am a radio personality. Every day, I'm hustling. I now have three jobs. No, I have three *careers*. A job is a temporary means to an end. A career is a lifestyle.

The beautiful part about this story is that program director who did not listen to my air check is the same person who had to negotiate my contract. I guess the Bible *was* right when it said, "The Lord will prepare a table before you in the presence of your enemies."

Our job is not to worry about who's sitting at the table. Our job is to eat.

Can you imagine the smile on my face and the confidence in my God when I sat across from her? This was the same lady who wouldn't give me the time of day a few months ago. Now, per Yolanda Adams' request, per Yo Yo's recommendation, she had to pay me and she still hadn't listened to my air check. It's cool. She can listen to me on the air!

To make matters worse for this poor woman, the Yolanda Adams Morning Show was getting ready to be syndicated into nine markets. Now, the show would not just be on locally in Houston, we would be on in Atlanta, Philadelphia, Charlotte, Raleigh Durham, Washington, D.C., Indianapolis, Richmond, and New York. This confirms that God is the best knower. He's in control!

I was so glad I got denied by the program director. Had she given me the job I'd dreamed up, I would likely have remained a local talent, but through God's temporary delay, ten years later, we are syndicated in over 50 markets!

Here's a blessing I received in the mail one day!

Dear Mr. Wiley:

I want to say thank you. During the winter snowstorm in Atlanta last year, my husband and I were unfortunately stuck in the house for a whole week with the kids. I remembered I had the videos your wonderful manager blessed me with.

We began to watch all 4 of those videos and I had never, in the 9 years of us being married, seen my husband laugh so hard!!!!!!

He watched those videos all week. On that Saturday he saw me getting ready to go to noon service (Berean Christian Church, Pastor Kerwin Lee) and he wanted to go. Marcus, my husband gave his life to Christ!!!! His words were, "That comedian made being saved look cool and fun." He said he was encouraged through your comedy to try God. My prayer to God was to have a laborer cross his path that he can identify Christ in them.

Thank you!!!! For the Grace of God in your life through your comedic gift!!! It's working!!!

Dee Conyers, Atlanta, GA

This, my friend, is what it's all about. You know you're in the perfect will of God when people start giving their lives to Christ as a result of you flowing your purpose!

People always ask me the question, "How did you get where you are today?" I don't look at it like I've made it, but I'm definitely making it! J.J. Watt, defensive end for the Houston Texans said, "Success is not owned, it's leased, and every day the rent is due!"

When I wake up in the morning, I thank God for another day to do something awesome. I thank Him for my life, health, and strength. I thank Him for being a perfect gentleman — opening doors for me. I ask for forgiveness, wisdom, and knowledge. I pray for my family, friends, and people who just don't understand. But as soon as I end the prayer... it's time to clock in!

ACKNOWLEDGEMENTS

I want to say thank you to EVERYBODY God has allowed me to meet. I appreciate your prayers, support, encouragement, inspiration, love, friendship, and all the other things that bring a tear to my eye.

In the words of Glen Jones... "We've only just begun!"